My Mimi Is a Freckle Detective

ISBN 979-8-89112-156-0 (Paperback)
ISBN 979-8-89112-158-4 (Hardcover)
ISBN 979-8-89112-157-7 (Digital)

Covenant Books
11661 Hwy 707
Murrells Inlet, SC 29576
www.covenantbooks.com

I Heard the Children Talking

My Mimi Is a Freckle Detective

Nurse Troy

My Mimi is not only my grandmom but a nurse who at work is
    called a freckle detective too!
She gets kids to help her as they and their parents learn something
    new.
As a freckle detective, she works with kids at a medical office,
And she says that we are the best. What do you call your grandmom?
    Where does she work?

When kids visit with her, they are there for a health checkup.
Of course, she talks to them too,
Telling them to be honest and not keep secrets, "Don't be scared."
To make sure all kids are healthy, she doesn't stop there.
She checks their whole bodies from their toes to their hair!

She looks for things that make us special in places that need to be
    seen,
Like checking for moles and birthmarks and everything in between!

The kids' parents are always there too, my Mimi would have it no
    other way,
And when the exam is finished, they all shout, "Hooray!"

The truth is my Mimi is a nurse practitioner.
Her know-how comes from years of working with all of us.

She explains all kinds of interesting things to kids without any fuss.
She teaches us about all the parts of our bodies,
From ankles to belly buttons and even eyelids!

There is so much to know because each part looks different, and
    none acts quite the same.
Our noses are for smelling and breathing in air, not for catching
    butterflies or Mardi Gras beads,
Our ears let us hear music or know when someone calls out our
    name!
Do you have a nickname you like being called?

Each part of our bodies is so precious when it was created,
We must always be careful of how each is treated.

Our bodies work hard all day making us bigger and stronger each
    day.
Let's see your muscles today!
All areas of the body should be respected, cared for, and cleaned.
Washing is mostly done by us privately in a shower or tub.

Genitals for girls and boys need a soaking each day,
And when asked if we need help, big kids simply say, "Thank you,"
    and "Nope."
We get to work cleaning all places with soap.

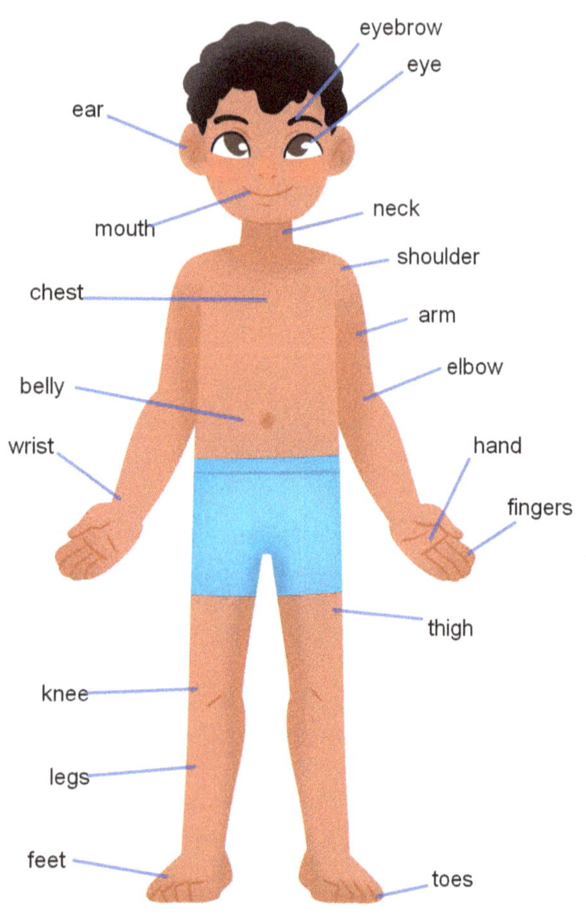

eyebrow
eye
ear
neck
shoulder
mouth
chest
arm
elbow
belly
wrist
hand
fingers
thigh
knee
legs
feet
toes

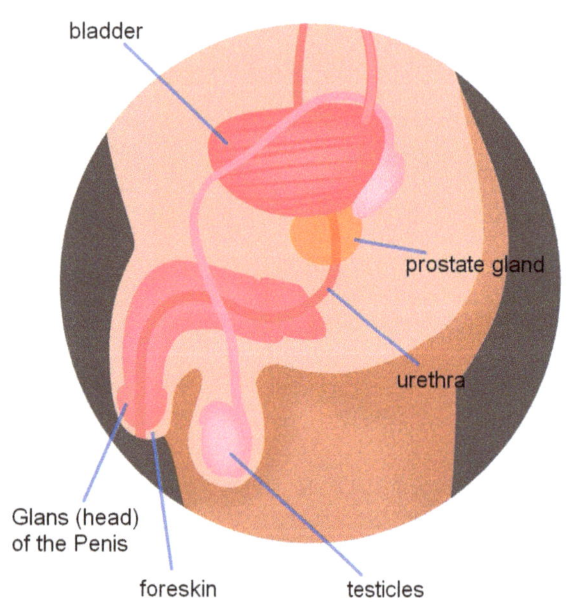

bladder
prostate gland
urethra
Glans (head)
of the Penis
foreskin
testicles

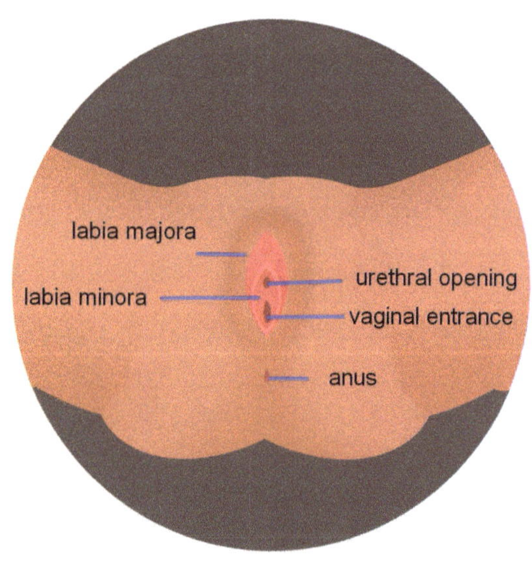

labia majora
labia minora
urethral opening
vaginal entrance
anus

My Mimi always tells kids to share how they are feeling,
To help understand what is appropriate and what might feel
    uncomfortable or need healing!

We know the right names and the whereabouts of each of our parts,
    for you see,
We don't have three different names for our elbows or our football-
    kicking knees.
It is important we know the names of our body parts because they
    are all special and good.

Boys have a penis with a urethra that urine (little kids say pee-pee)
    passes out.
This allows them to stand while urinating, but that's not what a girl
    will do.
We learned girls have a urethra too, but theirs is not outside of their
    body to see,
And we know, this is why they get to sit whenever they need to go
    potty.

The differences between boys and girls don't just stop there.
Girls have a vagina below their urethra that also needs care.

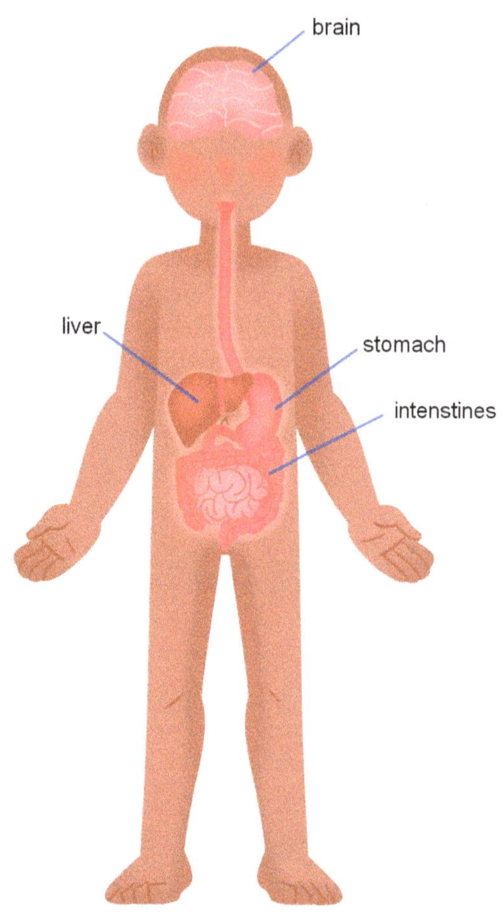

brain
liver
stomach
intenstines

Not all boys' and girls' body parts are different, and in fact, most
    are the same,
Like mouths, bellies, or buttocks, which kids who haven't been
    taught right will just call crazy names!
These are some of the parts that kids need to help them grow strong,
From the esophagus, stomach, intestines, and lungs, they all play a
    part in powering kids along.

Girls have another special part, their bodies sublime,
It's called the uterus, where babies grow for nine months before
    birth!
Babies grow in the uterus, and not in the stomach for sure.
Bellies are for taking in vitamins and minerals, from food we grow
    or bring home from the store.

Where does your food come from?
What is the healthiest food you like to eat?

Whether a body part is a boy's or a girl's, *all body parts* are private right from the start.

And so I ask you, kid to kid, can someone braid your eyebrow? How silly and heck no to the no!
Or decide to paint your toes while you sleep? How preposterous, we know!

It could be tickles or touching without permission,
If you feel uncomfortable, weird, or sad and can't explain the reason,
It is important to tell every grown-up you trust, no matter what the
    season.

Because if there is one thing to know,
When it comes to your body, *no always means no*!

Who would you tell in the summer?
Who could you tell during the school year?
Who could you tell on the weekends?

My Mimi wants all kids to know that their body is their own
    personal space,
And if we know what to look out for, we will be prepared for what
    we might face!

No one should hit, punch, or touch you,
As we all know this is something you don't do!
And none of us needs a spanking.
We are smart enough to learn without a yanking.

No one has the right to scare you or show you things we just
    shouldn't see,
Your eyes should never be shown videos or pictures,
That makes you scared or think, *That's yucky yuck!*
When you sleep at night, we want only happy thoughts.

What are your happy thoughts at bedtime?
What are your three wishes for your family?

From our heads to our toes, we are *all* beautiful creations from above.
And all of us, *yes*! Every one of us is so very easy to love!

We are each an amazing kid, and we each have a special reason for
    being here.
And *no one* is a mistake or not good enough, as we sometimes
    might fear!

Even when we get in trouble for a thing we say or do,
Remember there are *no* bad kids—simply wrong choices or decisions!
And there is absolutely nothing wrong with you!

It's okay to make mistakes as we are learning, and no one is perfect.
My Mimi tells me even grown-ups at times have trouble listening!

We all must keep learning from our actions as we grow,
Which means sometimes we must tell others we are sorry.
And it might not always be the easiest thing to do as you know.

How do you say sorry to people in your family?

Every single kid should be loved and appreciated,
As we are all special blessings from the day we are created!

What are your family blessings? Can you name a few?

My Mimi says she gets her strength from her faith.
Where does your family get their strength from?
What are your favorite things to do together?

From our pinky toes way up to our brains in our skull,
We know each body part is ours alone, and we treat them with love,

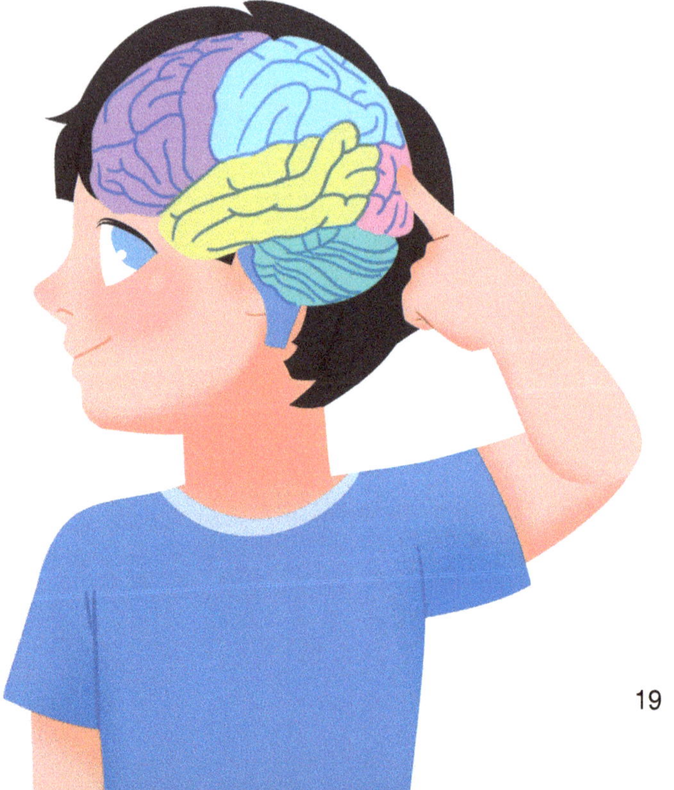

So we never take chances because a kid or adult tells us to do
something dangerous.

Can you think of some things that would be dangerous?
Do you wear a helmet when you ride your bike?

As we get older, we learn and celebrate how different we are in our own special way.
We will learn to love and be thankful for the body we've been given,
We respect that no two kids are the same in how we look, act, or even what we say and how we say it!

Could you imagine how boring the world would be if we all were
    the same and looked and sounded alike?
Do you know someone who speaks a different language than you?
Can you say words in another language? Or count?

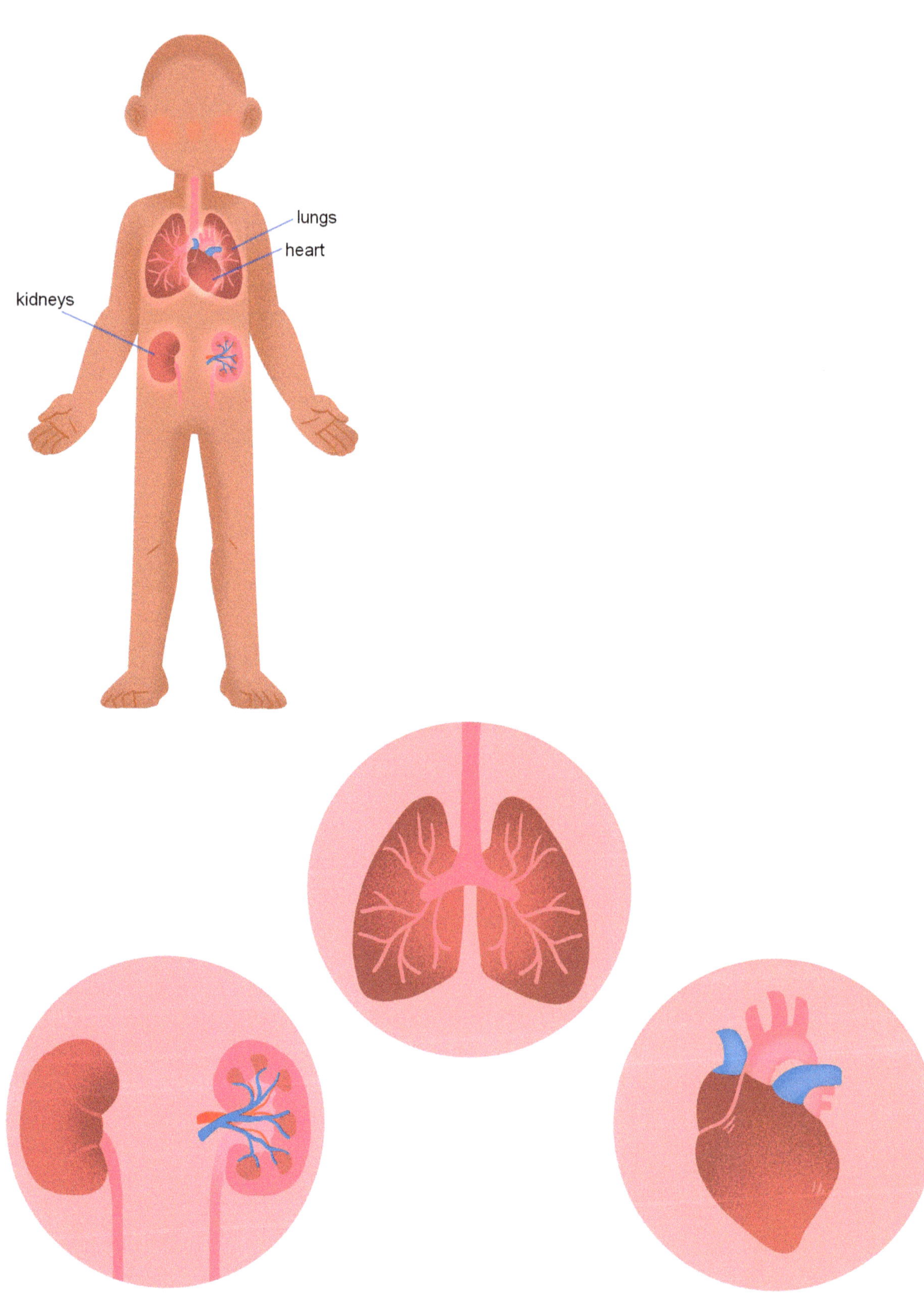

lungs
heart
kidneys

The different ways our bodies look is cause for celebration,
As no part of any body is ever gross, disgusting, bad, or cause for
   shaming or humiliation!

Each part is a gift that together creates our bodies' boundaries that
   we can see,
And no matter when or where we go, all our bodies deserve privacy!

What are your family's rules about privacy?

Do you like privacy when you are changing clothes or in the
   bathroom?

This means no unwanted touching or teasing as your body is your
    personal space.
Even if it seems playful at first—
You get to decide when you are not ready for a kiss or an embrace.

So speak up if something feels wrong or just not right!
As no secrets should be kept from the trusted grown-ups you hold
    tight.

I keep only good surprises like Mimi's present for her birthday, not
    secrets!
What are other good surprises in your family?

There are some days we just do not want a kiss and a hug,
And some days we want them aplenty!
Always everyone likes to be asked first,
To make sure we are immediately ready!

Can you think of a day you were not ready?
Who do you like to get hugs from?

So hooray! You are starting to learn about your body,
And how every single part of it is private and good.

If someone forgets all of these lessons you now know,
Talk loudly and tell them to stop on the double.
As this is your right as a kid, and talking about it will never get you
    in trouble.

And if some big kid doesn't know the lessons you've learned,
Talk loudly and tell them to stop on the double.
Telling important things to adults is never tattling or snitching; it
    is helping another.

Has anyone told you not to say something?
Who could you tell something serious to without them getting
    mad?

You deserve to *always* be protected, safe, and loved.
You are a joy to know, and your life has a wonderful purpose.

There is *no one* else in this whole wide world that is exactly like you!
So keep your amazing self with people who love you for you.
And remember it is our job as adults to keep you safe and help you
    understand all that is true.

What are some wonderful true things about you?
Who do you know that will never stop loving you?
Nurses and doctors and teachers like Mimi are everywhere to help
    keep us safe!
What do you want to do when you grow up?
You could be a nurse practitioner helping kids too!

How to Use the Book for Parents and Teachers

Research has shown that warnings about good touch and bad touch will not equip children to disclose sexual abuse if it occurs or prevent it from happening. Most perpetrators of abuse are known to the child and trusted by the adults, as part of calculated grooming put in place prior to any boundary violations of a child. Abusive touch can feel "tingling," albeit sad and unwanted. Parents' warnings to "tell me if anything happens" fade into the confusion and unwarranted shame and guilt children feel. The program Darkness to Light stresses the importance of adults eliminating opportunities for one adult to be alone with children. This book is meant to be read with children to facilitate the child's comfort with language about their body to enable them to speak of any concerns that arise. In the clinic, I have children laughing as we discuss not putting Mardi Gras beads in their noses. They cannot retain a lesson on body safety if the teaching induces fear.

There are three points I tell every family. The first is that *vagina* and *penis* are not bad words. We show our discomfort when we use nicknames that will not enable a child to tell a teacher a proper anatomical site has been touched. Children outcrying that their "cookie" was "messed with" may not be adequately responded to by a caring adult. We do not have different words for other body parts, so children might feel ashamed and embarrassed or correctly assess discomfort in those who should be their first line of information, so they seek education from their variously informed peers. The second family rule of not keeping secrets is essential as perpetrators, through threats or building special relationships, will engage a child in a promise of not telling. We want children who can state, "I get to tell my parents everything." Family surprises can be kept for short periods of time when special occasions are approaching but never "secrets," the language of abusers. The third rule is that corporal punishment should not happen in a home, but there are consequences for actions; however, they never involve physical pain. Discipline means to teach. If we cannot self-regulate our anger in giving consequences, we are not modeling self-regulation. Research has shown physical punishment does not work and raises the stress hormones in children, making it more difficult for them to control their emotions. Additionally, perpetrators of child abuse can scare a child into silence by threatening, "You will get a whipping if they find out what you did." We want to raise children who can answer, "I never get hit, and I'm telling." Parenting classes can be found at children's hospitals. Every generation has to get a little better based on the current understanding of child development.

A final note: If you have experienced child abuse in any form, it was never your fault. Great strides in counseling have improved our response to children and adults receiving the healing they deserve. Trauma-focused cognitive behavioral therapy is an evidence-based therapy for resolving the pain of abuse. Putting a Band-Aid over a wound or saying we will not talk about it anymore does not resolve the issues that can be energy-draining, at the least if not addressed. Be as courageous as the children I care for every day. Tell your truth, and give yourself the gift of true freedom.

If you require more information, start with your children's hospital CAC (Child Advocacy Centers) and read about adverse childhood experiences and how to heal.

Anne Troy PhD, FNP-BC, APRN, SANE
Associate Professor of Nursing
Forensic NP
atroy@uhcno.edu

About the Author

Nurse Troy is a forensic nurse practitioner who has assessed thousands of children after childhood abuse. After forty-five years in the community working to end the epidemic of childhood suffering at the hands of people often known and trusted by the children, she has written her teaching points in a child-friendly presentation. This book can be used by parents to empower their own children in a nonthreatening manner. Good touch, bad touch teachings confuse young children. Nurse Troy has provided safety rules to families that allow open communication and diminish the shame and self-blame that often accompany intergenerational abuses to children. Her mental health background and doctoral studies have guided her approach to safety tips for parents, providing them with evidence-based means of remediation from their own previously unspoken past trauma. Nurse Troy is a full-time associate professor of nursing at the University of Holy Cross in New Orleans and a mimi to six grandchildren, the oldest contributing art and inspiration to the book.